How to be a

Pirate

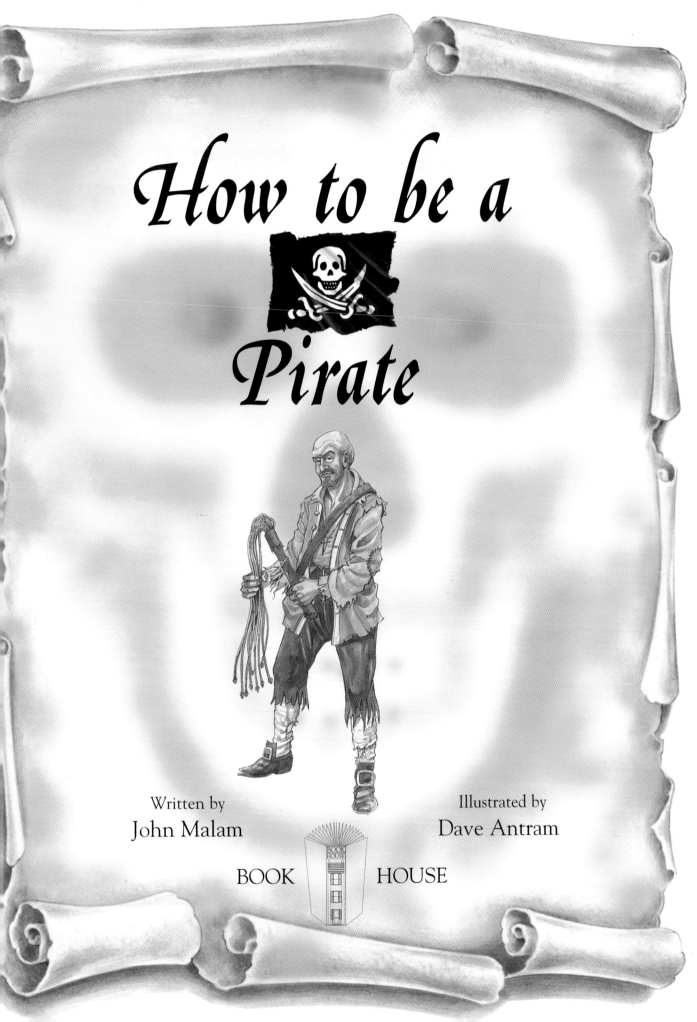

Written by
John Malam

Illustrated by
Dave Antram

BOOK HOUSE

John Malam studied ancient history and archaeology at the University of Birmingham, after which he worked as an archaeologist at the Ironbridge Gorge Museum, Shropshire. He is now a writer, editor and reviewer specialising in books for children.

Dave Antram was born in Brighton in 1958. He studied at Eastbourne College of Art and then worked in advertising for 15 years before becoming a full-time artist. He has illustrated many children's non-fiction books.

Series created and designed by **David Salariya**
Editor **Karen Barker Smith**
Fact Consultant **Stuart Slade**, Education Officer at the National Maritime Museum in London

Published in Great Britain in 2005 by
Book House, an imprint of
The Salariya Book Company Ltd
25 Marlborough Place, Brighton BN1 1UB

Please visit the Salariya Book Company at:
www.salariya.com

ISBN 1-904642-41-1
A catalogue record for this book is available from the British Library.
The Salariya Book Company operates an environmentally friendly policy wherever possible.
Printed and bound in China.

Photographic credits
t=top b=bottom c=centre l=left r=right

The Art Archive / Château-Musée de Dieppe / Dagli Orti: 15
The Art Archive / Museum für Völkerkunde Vienna / Dagli Orti: 21l
© National Maritime Museum, London: 18, 19, 21r, 28

Every effort has been made to trace copyright holders. The Salariya Book Company apologises for any unintentional omissions and would be pleased, in such cases, to add an acknowledgement in future editions.

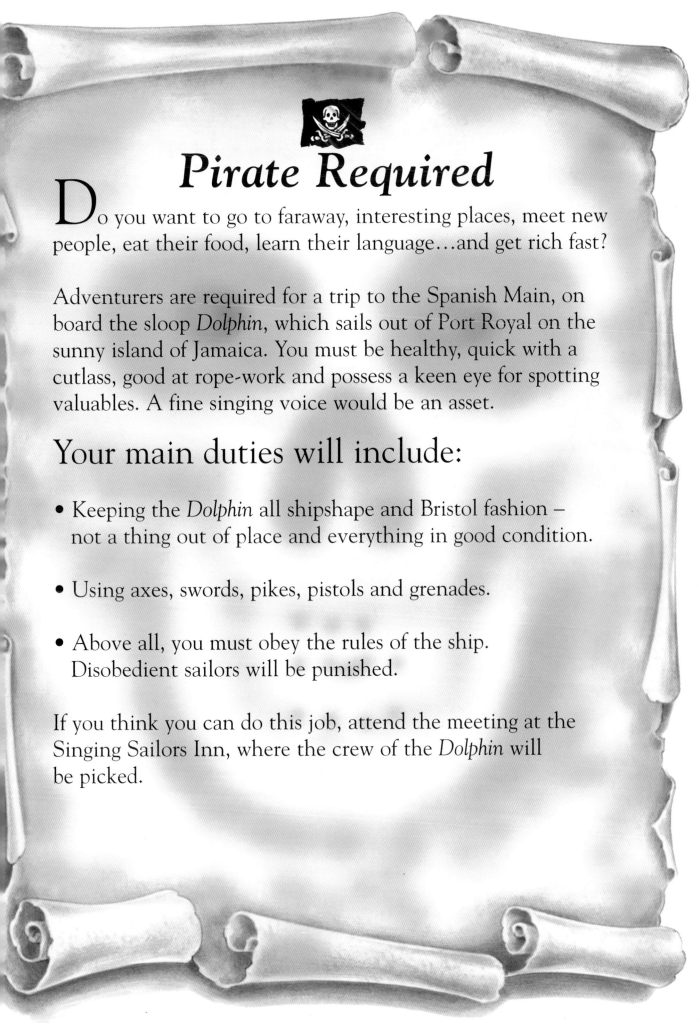

Pirate Required

Do you want to go to faraway, interesting places, meet new people, eat their food, learn their language…and get rich fast?

Adventurers are required for a trip to the Spanish Main, on board the sloop *Dolphin*, which sails out of Port Royal on the sunny island of Jamaica. You must be healthy, quick with a cutlass, good at rope-work and possess a keen eye for spotting valuables. A fine singing voice would be an asset.

Your main duties will include:

- Keeping the *Dolphin* all shipshape and Bristol fashion – not a thing out of place and everything in good condition.
- Using axes, swords, pikes, pistols and grenades.
- Above all, you must obey the rules of the ship. Disobedient sailors will be punished.

If you think you can do this job, attend the meeting at the Singing Sailors Inn, where the crew of the *Dolphin* will be picked.

Contents

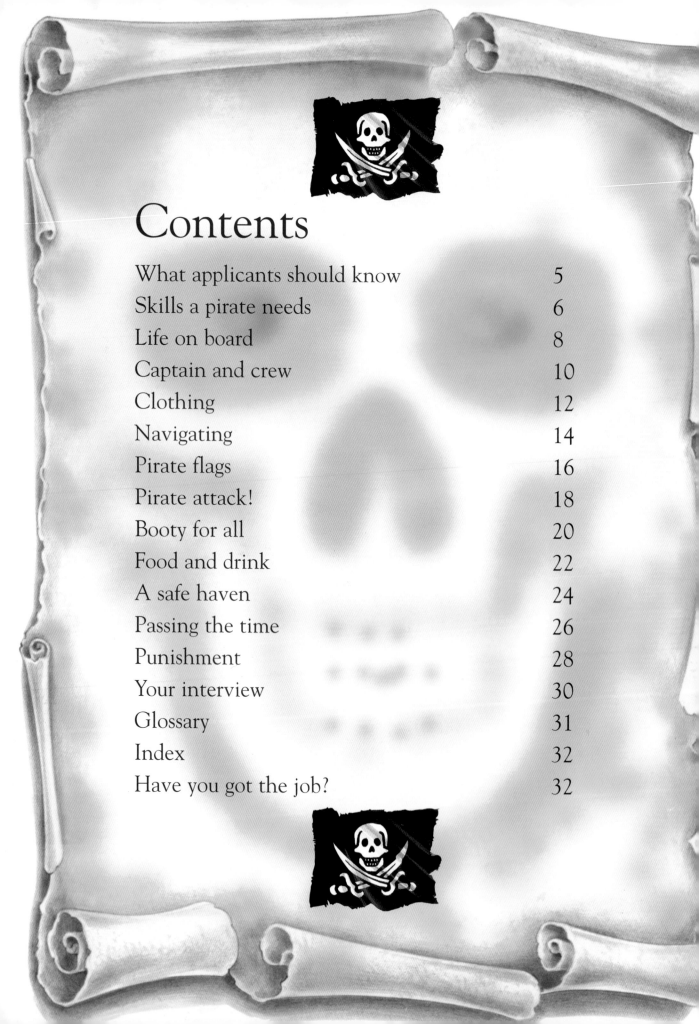

What applicants should know

So you think you have what it takes to be a pirate? Be prepared for a dangerous journey – the islands of the Caribbean Sea might have sun, sand and shimmering silver, but you're not going there for a holiday! It is around the year 1700, and you'll be going to a part of the New World where every last scoundrel, thief and drunk has fled. Port Royal, on the south coast of Jamaica, is where the *Dolphin* sails from. It is a safe haven for pirates and all who live outside the law. It has become the major city in the region with a population of about 3,000. Port Royal is sheltered from storms. On fair days ships leave her deep harbour for the Spanish Main. This is the name given to the area that stretches from the north coast of South America to Florida in North America.

The Caribbean Sea, 1680

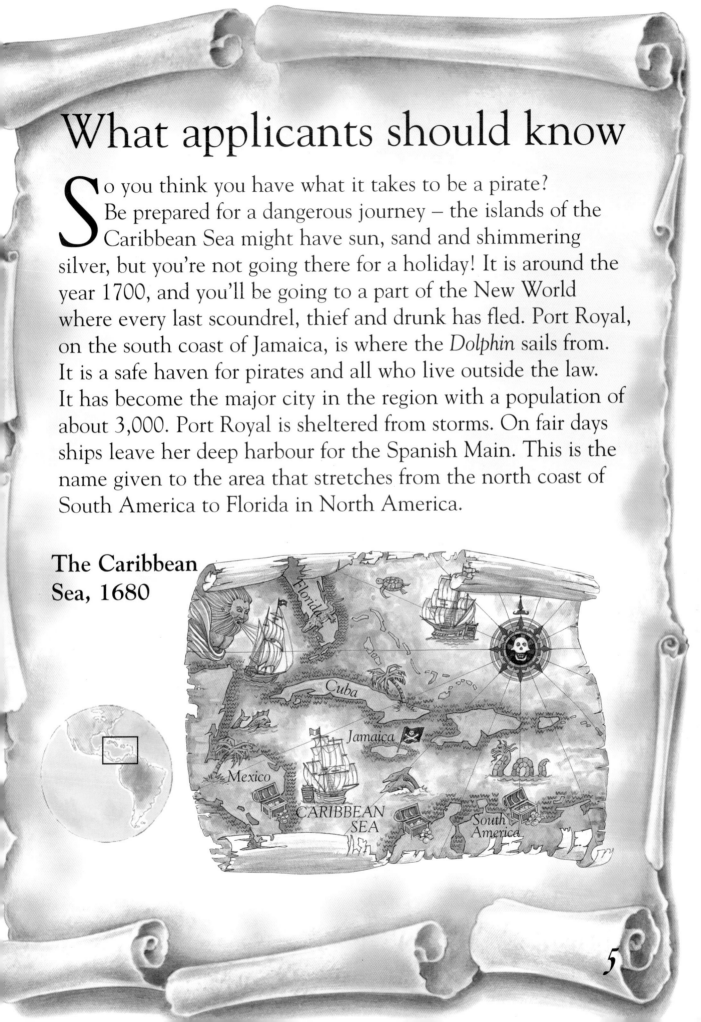

Florida
Cuba
Jamaica
Mexico
CARIBBEAN SEA
South America

Skills a pirate needs

Living on a ship doesn't suit everyone. Think hard before you decide to set your sea-legs on board the *Dolphin*. Once she's at sea there's no turning back until her hold is filled with treasure. It's tough work keeping the ship in good condition, day and night. Be prepared to go without sleep until your work is done. When a ship is attacked and taken, you'll need all your courage to protect yourself and win the fight.

Head for heights?

▲ You'll need to be brave and have a firm grip to climb the rigging in all weathers and to act as the look-out.

Tying knots

▶ Knots are important on board – they can join two pieces of rope together, make loops, or tie things to parts of the ship.

A bowline makes the best loop – it won't slip.

Never a moment to spare

▲ Life is often very busy onboard ship – one minute you could be sewing sailcloth, the next you might be busy with rope-work, tying a bowline knot at the end of a mooring rope, or using bend knots to join ropes together.

Start
Finish

Bowline knot for making loops

Rowing and sword-fighting

▼ You'll need strong arms and a straight back to row the ship's boat towards another ship. The harder you row, the sooner you will reach your prize.

Only if you get it right!

▼ Once aboard the prize ship you must fight with your cutlass. This is a heavy sword with a short sharp blade and a basket-shaped guard to protect your hand and wrist. Use it for slashing and hacking at the enemy.

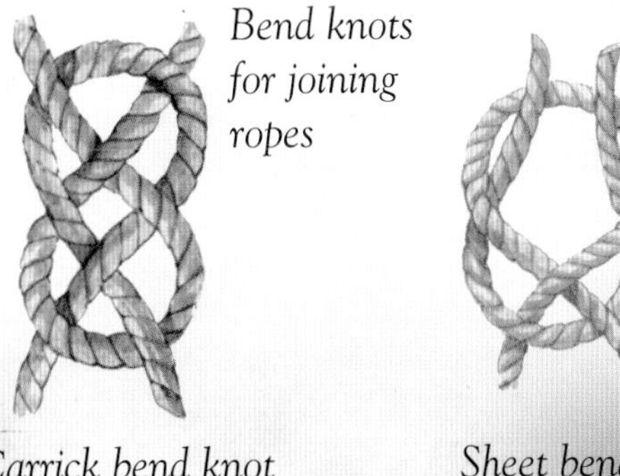

Bend knots for joining ropes

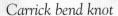

Carrick bend knot

Sheet bend knot

Life on board

You might be at sea for weeks before you sight a prize ship. Until then, your life will consist of routine, boring jobs. Singing shanties (pirate songs) will help pass the time. You'll lift the crew's spirits if you can whistle a tune on a pipe. Everyone has a job to do: repairing the deck, pouring molten lead to make musket balls or preparing fresh fish to eat. The gold and riches you seek are never forgotten, though.

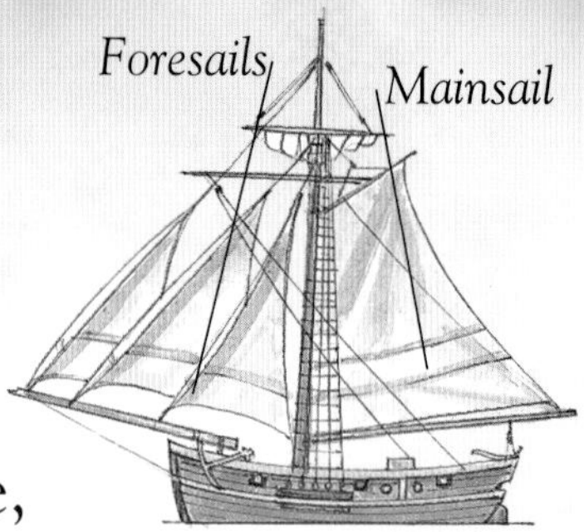
Foresails
Mainsail

Pirate sloop

◀ Many Caribbean pirates sail in fast ships called sloops. They have a single mast with a large mainsail and smaller foresails.

Sing along men... We're off to seek our fortune, lads...
Only one more day together...

A cat hunting rats on board ship

Treasure ship

◀ Keep a close watch for a prize – a slow-sailing galleon bound for Spain. It's cargo will be treasure from places like Peru and Mexico.

Keeping water out

▼ The ship is leaking! Don't panic, all wooden ships let in water through small gaps in their hulls. It collects in the ship's bilges and stinks of rot and filth. Pumps suck it up and pour it into buckets or over the side of the ship.

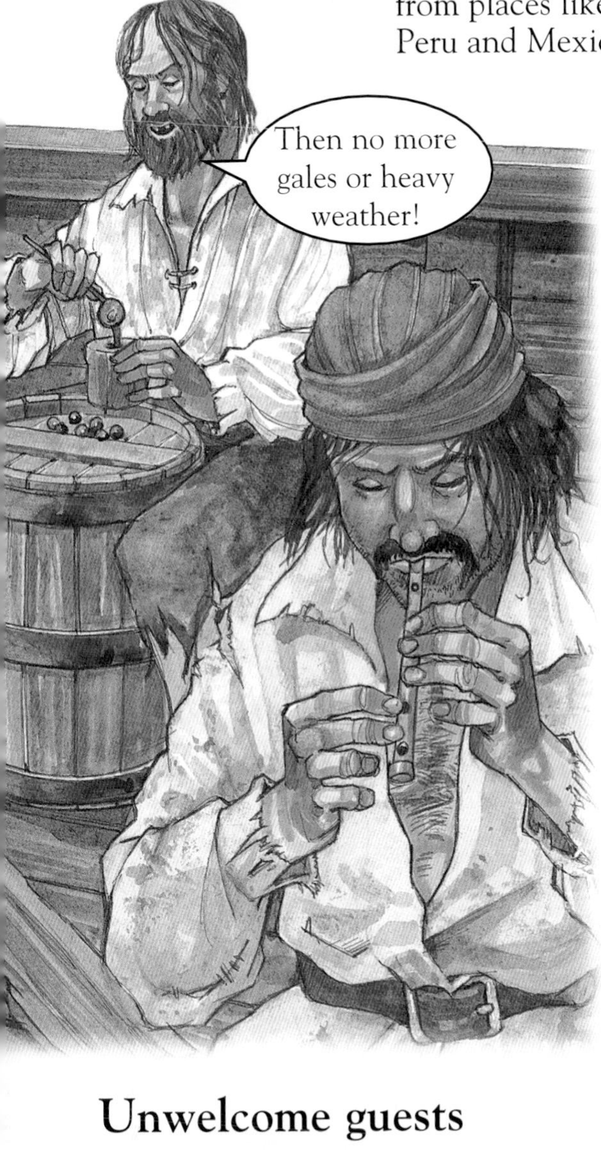
Then no more gales or heavy weather!

Bilge pump

▼ One never-ending job is caulking timbers. This means pushing shredded rope, called oakum, into gaps in the hull. It is then glued in place with black pitch, which sets hard to make a water-tight seal.

Ramming iron
Caulking mallet

Unwelcome guests

◀ On some ships there are more rats than seamen. They gnaw their way through ropes and timbers, eat the crew's food and spread disease. The ship's cats kill many, but if you see a rat, toss it to the sharks.

Captain and crew

The Captain expects every seaman to know his place and do his duty the best he can. In return for hard work and loyalty you will get a share of any treasure taken. The size of your share depends on the job you do. There will be no arguments about it, since you must keep to the rules you signed when you joined the ship.

Your Captain

▼ He is the ship's commander. He gives orders during battle and decides which way to set the ship's course. He's been voted Captain because the crew look up to him as a strong leader.

Cutlass

Choosing the Captain

▼ Before a ship sails, the crew votes which one of them should be Captain. Scuffles may break out, but one man is finally chosen. He promises riches for all.

Vote me Cap'n, lads, an' I'll make ye all rich!

Carpenter
Surgeon
Seaman
Cabin boy
Musician

Deposing the Captain

If at any time the Captain shows signs of weakness, such as refusing to attack a prize ship or cruelty towards his men, he can be deposed (voted out). Then the crew choose another man as Captain.

You can have my vote!
I'd rather have a rat as my Cap'n!

Cook
Boatswain
Master gunner
Seamen

The Quartermaster

▶ The Quartermaster is second-in-command and takes charge of the rations and captured booty. He is the only man allowed to flog (whip) a seaman. This is usually done with a cat-o'-nine-tails – a whip with nine knotted lashes.

Cat-o'-nine-tails

The Ship's Articles

▼ Every seaman must sign the Ship's Articles (below) and swear on the Holy Bible to obey the rules. Brawling, cheating at cards and cowardice are forbidden. The rules also state how the treasure is to be shared.

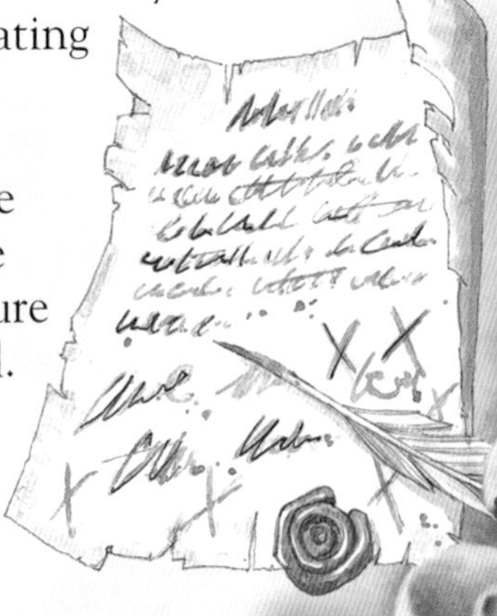

Clothing

You are likely to own only one set of clothes. You'll work, fight and sleep in them. New clothes are expensive, and the only way you'll get clothes like a rich man is by stealing some from a wealthy seafarer. Like the other seamen on board, your clothes will be made of heavy wool, cotton, or perhaps stitched together from scraps of canvas sailcloth. You will also be barefoot. You will wear loose-fitting trousers rolled up or cut off below the knee, and a thigh-length shirt or coat.

Sailcloth for clothes

▼ Sailcloth is a thick, rough canvas woven from hemp fibres. Old pieces of sailcloth can be used to make hard-wearing clothes.

This sail has more holes than my shirt.

◀ Before you board a prize ship, give your clothes a thick coating of black tar. Your enemy's sword will slip off the tar. This will save your skin.

Keeping clean

Fresh water is for drinking, not for washing clothes or bodies. If you want to wash yourself, use rainwater collected in tubs. If the ship drops anchor, take a dip in the sea – but beware of sharks.

This water's filthier than me!

Fashion

Although pirates wear hoops in their ears, made of brass or even gold, they sell most of the jewellery they capture from their enemies.

Rags and riches

Cocked hat with a feather
Leather strap for holding weapons
Velvet jacket
Silk sash
Trousers tied at the knee
Stockings
Silver-buckled shoes

▲ The Captain has fine clothes, taken from his enemies.

▶ Your clothes are canvas rags, smeared in black tar to protect you from the cold and wet. You will wear them until they rot away. If you lose a leg in a fight, a carpenter will carve a wooden peg that you can strap to your stump.

Navigating

The navigator uses the best tools available to find the ship's position at sea. In the daytime he measures the height of the sun in relation to the horizon. At night, the moon and stars help him to fix the ship's course. By knowing where the ship is, the direction of her course can be worked out and plotted on charts. Many of the sailors on board are expert navigators, but it is the Captain who decides where the ship sails.

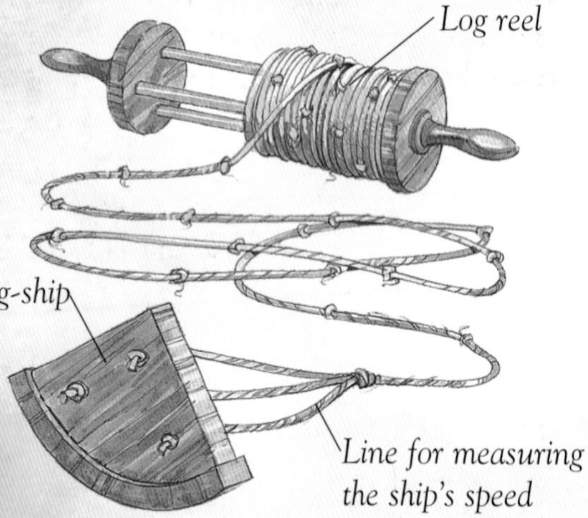
Log reel
Log-ship
Line for measuring the ship's speed

▲ Speed at sea is measured in knots. A knotted line (above) is unwound over the side. By measuring the number of knots which unwind in thirty seconds, the speed of the ship can be measured.

The anchor

▶ To stop the ship, her iron anchor is dragged along the seabed until it catches on a rock or sturdy object. In heavy weather, a firm anchor can stop the ship running aground.

Our course is straight and true.
Land Ho!

▲ Each day the Captain plots the ship's position on a chart. With his dividers he measures the distance sailed from day to day (above), to check that all is well with the course.

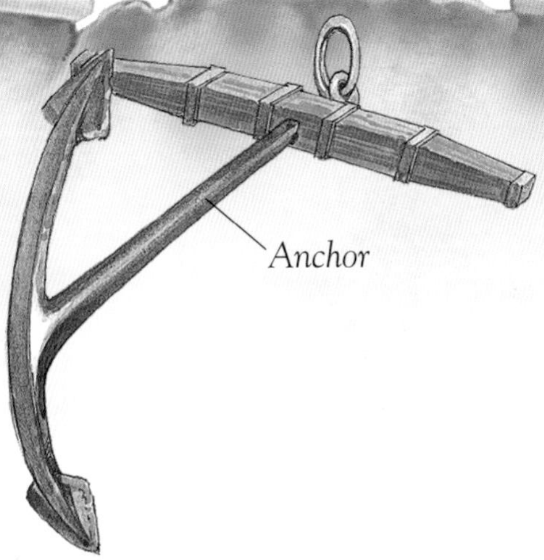
Anchor

Navigation tools

▼ You must always watch for rocks and other dangers. In fog, a sailor will lower a lead weight to the seabed to measure the water depth in fathoms. A fathom is the length between his outstretched arms – 1.83 m.

Another ten leagues to land.

▼ Other instruments include the compass for finding direction and the Captain's telescope, which allows him to see land and ships from a great distance. The dividers measure distance on the charts, and the backstaff is used by the navigator to work out the ship's position. Often, navigational tools are stolen from captured ships.

A 17th-century compass

Pirate flags

Be proud of the flag the *Dolphin* flies as she engages an enemy ship – the Jolly Roger. The flag's skull and crossbones are symbols understood by seamen of all nations. They stand for death and violence. Many a prize ship surrenders without a fight as soon as it spies the Jolly Roger at the top of the main mast.

A flag to fear

▼ If you're asked to make a Jolly Roger, the Captain will tell you what design he wants. The bolder the design, the more it will frighten your enemy.

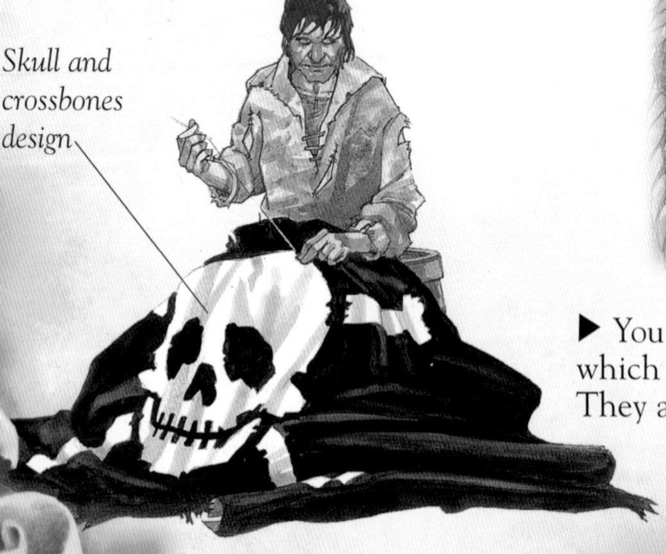
Skull and crossbones design

Raising the Jolly Roger

▼ In most battles, surprise is the best tactic – your ship wouldn't stand a chance in open battle. Wait until the last moment to raise your flag. Your enemy will not know whether you are friend or foe until it is too late.

Now you know who we are!

▶ You will see vessels called 'privateers', which fly the flags of their countries. They are private warships. Their governments give them permission to attack and plunder enemy ships, so they are really just pirates like you.

Your prize is in sight

▼ When your enemy finally sees the Jolly Roger flying from the main mast, she may try to escape. But your sloop, the *Dolphin*, is small and fast and you will soon be alongside her.

Different Jolly Rogers

◀ The skull and crossbones. A red background means all your enemies will die.

◀ The flag of John Rackham, known as 'Calico Jack' because he wore striped trousers.

◀ The flag of Edward Teach, known as 'Blackbeard'.

◀ The flag of Henry Every, known as 'Long Ben'. He raided ships in the Red Sea and Indian Ocean.

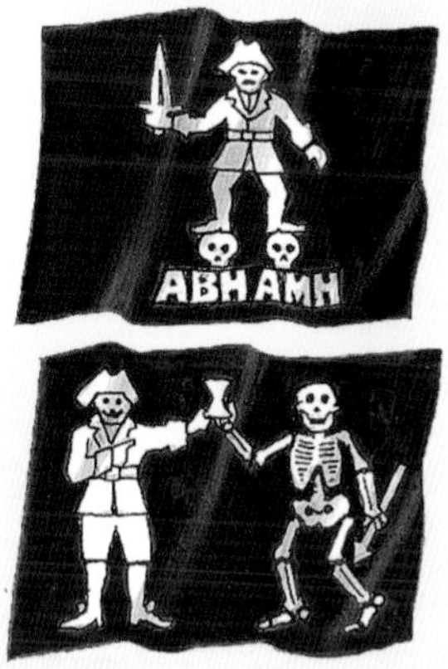
ABH AMH

◀ The two flags of Bartholomew Roberts. The letters on the top flag are the initials of men against whom he has vowed revenge. On the bottom flag a skeleton hands an hour glass to his prey, to show that time is running out.

Flags of other nations

Britain

France

Spain

Pirate attack!

Now the prize ship has seen your Jolly Roger she knows the *Dolphin* is a pirate ship. The next few minutes will be dangerous, as you board the ship and come face to face with your enemy. Some of them may turn against their own officers and change sides, hoping for a share of the ship's riches. The seamen who resist you will meet a bloody end, killed by a sword, axe or gun. Pirates are not known for their mercy.

Grenades

◀ Light the fuse, throw it, take cover and wait for the grenade to explode, flinging lead shot in every direction.

Avast, ye Spaniards!
Have mercy upon us!

Guns at sea

▼ When you're in action you must keep your gunpowder dry. You will use a flintlock musket when shooting from a distance and a flintlock pistol for close combat. Both weapons shoot heavy balls of lead, but the pistol can also be used for clubbing your enemies.

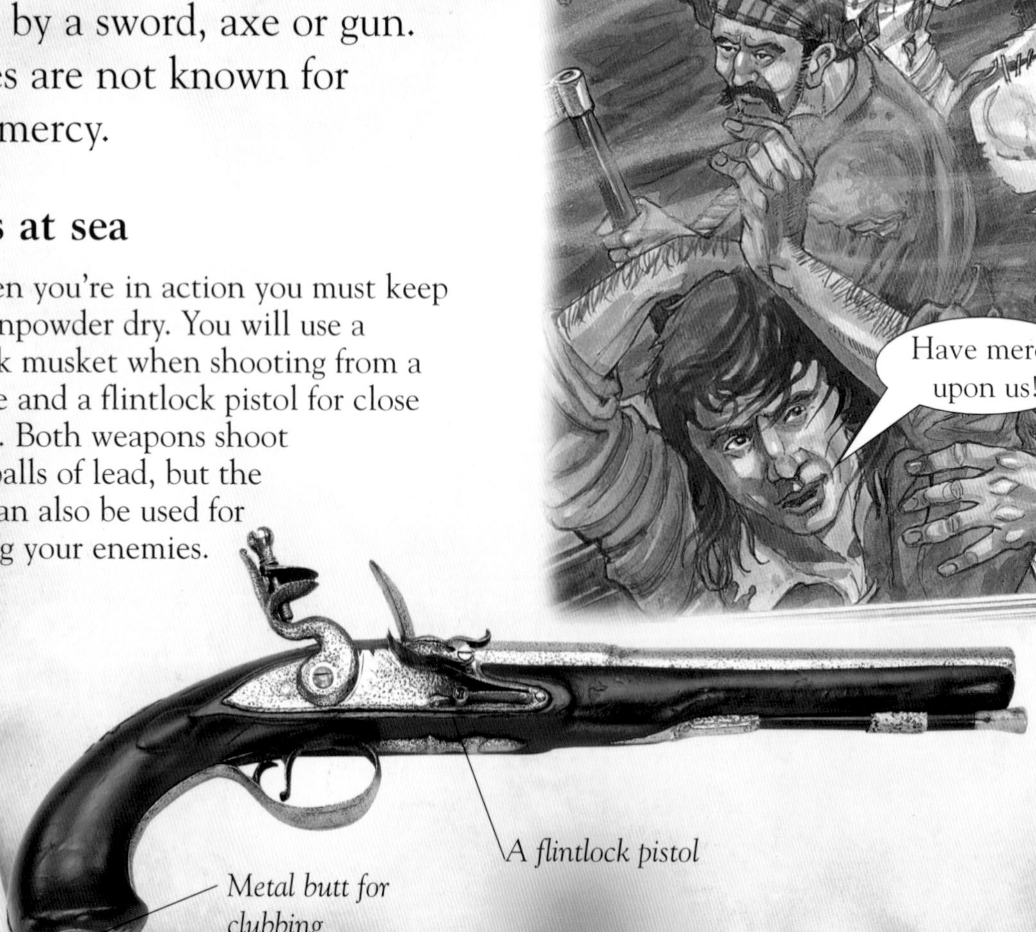

Metal butt for clubbing

A flintlock pistol

Cannonballs joined by chain

Chain-shot

◀ Chain-shot is fired into an enemy's rigging. With torn sails, a ship is dead in the water.

No booty, no reward!

Firing a cannon

▼ Sloops like the *Dolphin* carry small cannons which are used just to frighten the enemy – the last thing you want to do is sink the prize before you have plundered it! It takes three men to operate a cannon, firing one iron cannonball every ten minutes over a distance of about 150 m.

▼ In hand-to-hand fighting use axes, swords, daggers and pikes (like spears). Keep their blades and points sharp to cut through your enemy's tough leather clothes.

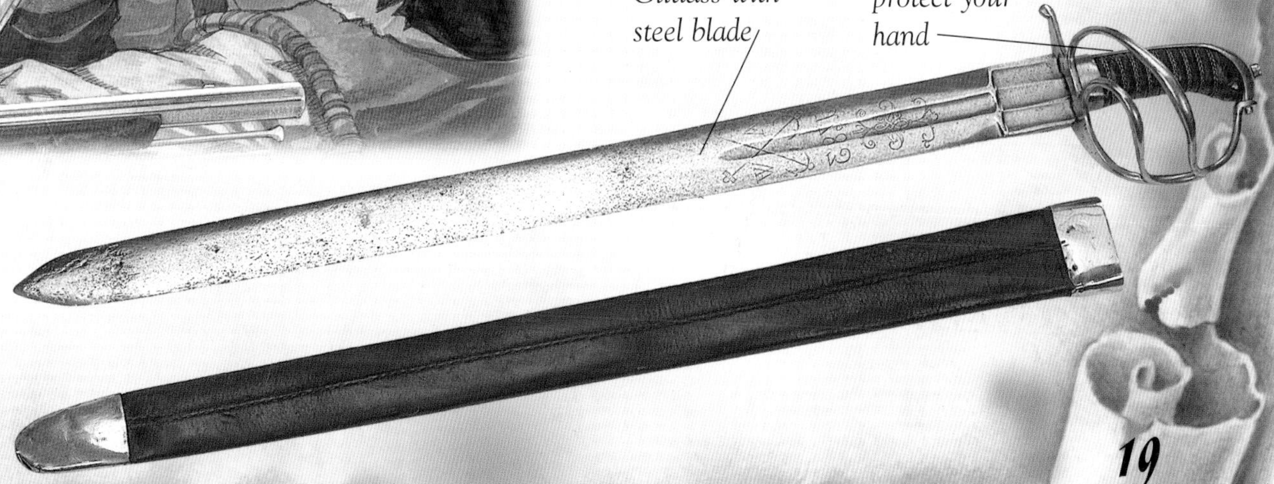

Cutlass with steel blade

Basket hilt to protect your hand

Booty for all

With an enemy ship under your control, it's time to find out what treasure she carries. The ship may contain chests of gold, silver coins, jewellery or other cargo you can steal. The Quartermaster will take charge of whatever booty is found. He will share it amongst the seamen, according to the Ship's Articles, at the end of the voyage and not before.

▲ Pirates look after each other. If you lose a limb, or get injured, you'll be given an extra share of the booty to make up for your loss.

Stealing provisions

▼ Take gunpowder to add to your supplies and any weapons you can find. Fresh water and food are always welcome, especially alcohol and tobacco.

Precious metal

▶ The Spanish took gold objects from the peoples of the New World. They melted them down to make coins and these were sent back to Europe on ships.

Medicine

◀ A medicine chest with potions ointments, oils, and doctor's tools could save your life – take it too!

The ultimate prize

▼ The greatest prize of all may well be the enemy ship herself. Any members of her crew who do not agree to join you will be cast adrift in a ship's boat. The Quartermaster will take command, and the ship will sell for a good price.

You'll find no more valuables on my ship.
Stop your lies, Captain!

▼ If your prize is a galleon from the Spanish treasure fleet, her hold may be full of coins. Look for gold doubloons and silver pesos. A peso is worth eight reales ('royals') so pirates call them 'pieces-of-eight'.

Gold lip-plug from Peru

CAROLUS·IIII·DEI·GRATIA·1795·

A silver 'piece-of-eight'

Food and drink

The *Dolphin* carries a good supply of food and drink, hopefully. Enough food at least until you take on new supplies at port, or seize a ship and raid its stores. Fresh food doesn't last long at sea. Even dried food turns bad in the damp air of the ship's hold. Only heavily salted fish and meat will last the length of the trip and you'll soon get bored of that. Cook will do his best to hide the bad taste with spices and make strongly flavoured drinks to wash your meals down.

Bottled beer

◀ Fresh water soon turns foul on a long voyage, so the ship carries bottles of beer for the crew to drink with their food.

What foul poison do you call this, Cook?

A turtle is killed with a wooden club

▲ Live sea turtles are kept in the hold until needed for food. They are put on their backs so they can't move around. Their meat is often grilled over a smoky fire.

Scurvy

If you're at sea for many weeks you will not eat many vegetables or much fresh fruit. This means you run the risk of scurvy – a disease caused by a lack of vitamin C. Watch out for these symptoms: blotches and sores on the skin, pimples on the gums, teeth falling out and feeling weak.

Rum ration

▶ You'll get a daily swig of rumbullion, a sweet alcohol made from Caribbean sugar. The English call it 'rum'.

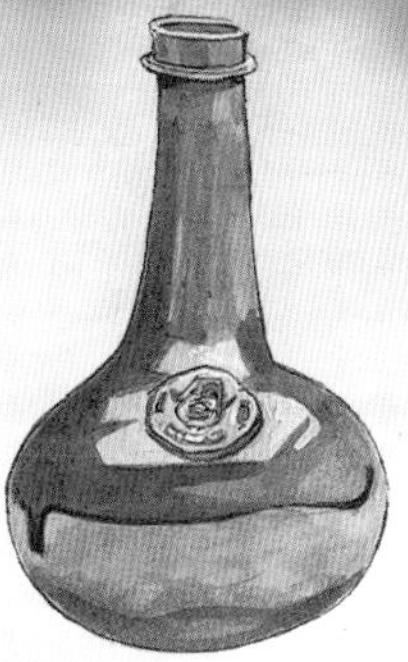

A pirate's menu

▼ The *Dolphin* sails with goats, caged hens which provide fresh meat and eggs. Fresh fish can be caught from the sea too, but on days when there is no fresh food, you must chew on ship's biscuits. These are known as 'hard tack' because they're so tough. Don't complain if you find a maggot in them (they eat the biscuits too).

It's barbecued sea turtle. Eat it and be grateful!

Caged hens
Hard tack
Salmagundi spiced stew

▶ Salamagundi is a stew made from roast meat (turtle, duck, hen or pigeon), chopped into chunks and soaked in wine. Vegetables (cabbage and onions) and occasionally fruit (mangoes) are thrown in and vinegar, salt, garlic, pepper and mustard are added. It's spicy!

A safe haven

Like many other pirate ships of the Spanish Main, the *Dolphin* regards the lawless Jamaican town of Port Royal as her home port. The town has many wealthy merchants who will buy your looted gold, silver and jewellery cheaply. They will sell it in London for a high price and with their profits they buy supplies of food and other goods to sell to pirates in Port Royal.

Life's luxuries

▲ You can afford to enjoy life now. Ask for a bottle of fine wine, but check that the cork is well tied on or else the contents could be sour.

Smoking allowed

▶ You can't smoke while you're on board ship for fear of setting it on fire – you have to make do with chewing tobacco instead. But when in port you can light up your clay pipe and smoke all day.

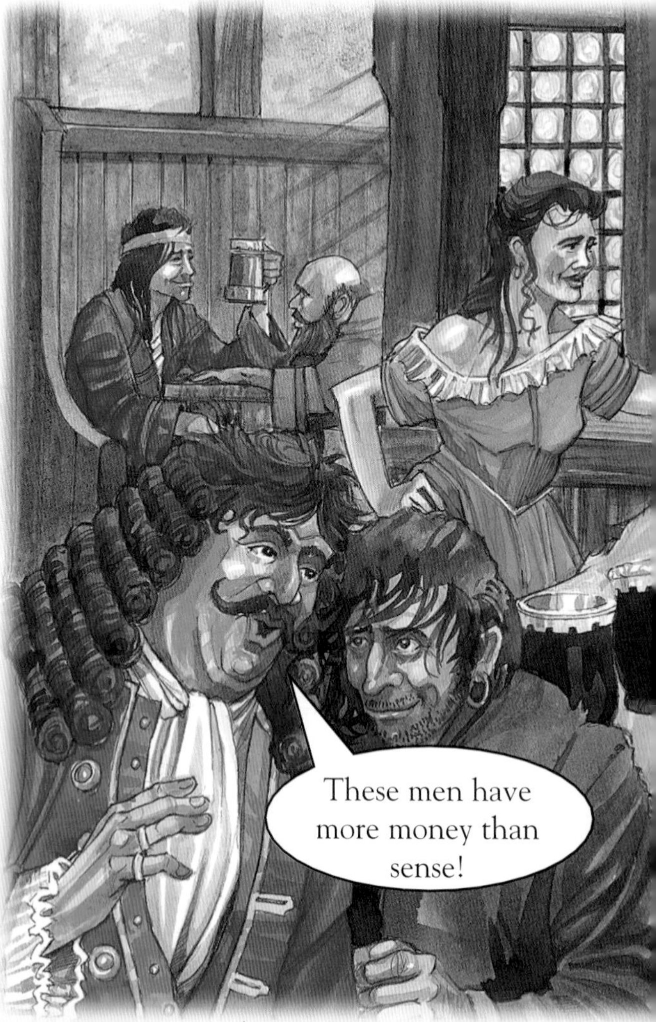
These men have more money than sense!

▲ You'll be welcome in the port's taverns, where you'll find entertainment to suit every seaman. But be warned. These places are filled with thieves and tricksters – both men and women – who will want your money.

Clay tobacco pipe

Drink and be merry!

What to do with your money

▼Cheats will try to swindle you out of your money at cards. They use weighted dice and a marked pack. Unless you catch them at it, you'll never know you've been tricked.

Sworn to secrecy

▼ You've heard stories that pirates sometimes bury their booty, but you tend to spend all of your captured wealth.

Passing the time

There's a lot of hard work to do on board the *Dolphin* – but you will have some time to relax and enjoy yourself. You could practise your skills as an artist, a singer, a dancer or a musician. Or you could let a fellow seaman give you a tattoo. You might even catch up on some much needed sleep. While the Captain sleeps in his private cabin, you'll sleep on the deck, or in the hold amongst the ship's equipment. Your bed will be a hammock or a straw mattress.

Now hop on your left foot.
Easier said than done, mate!

Keeping busy at sea

▶ Some of the men scratch pictures on to animal bones or teeth. Black soot rubbed over the marks makes them stand out.

Whale tooth

Dancing the night away

▲ Anyone for a dance? At the end of the day, when your work is done, musicians strike up a lively tune on the fiddle and the squeeze-box. They will play a dance tune with steps that are easy to learn.

Settling an argument

◀ Be prepared to settle an argument with your bare knuckles. While you fight, the rest of the ship's crew will be betting on who they think will win, even though the Ship's Articles forbid gambling.

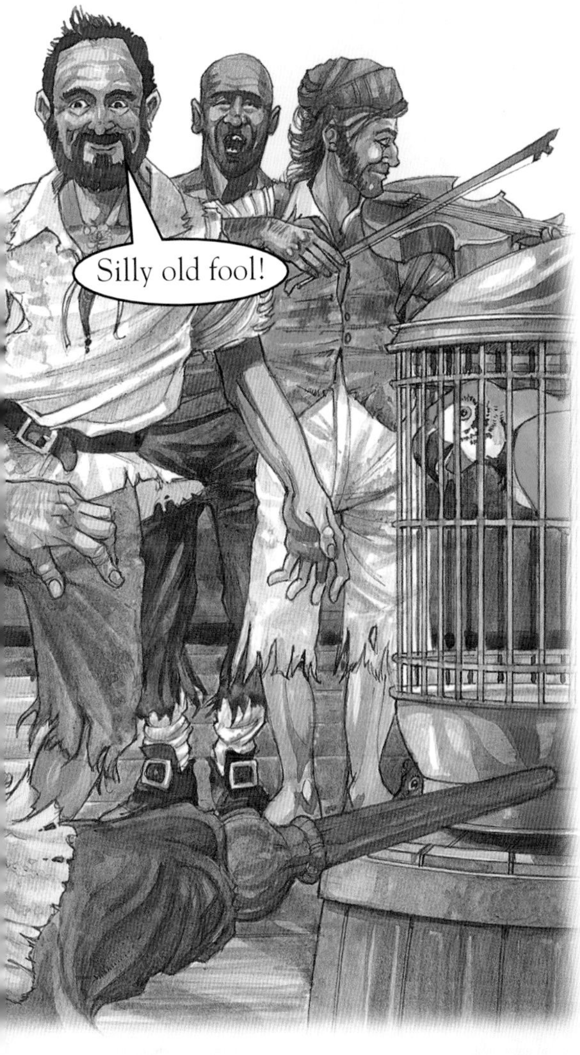
Silly old fool!

Tattooing

▶ Some seamen decorate their skin with pictures by pricking it with needles. Then they rub pigments (colours) into the designs. As the skin heals, a coloured picture is left under the skin.

Exotic creatures

▼ Macaws can be taught to speak.

The exotic animals of the New World make excellent companions on board ship.

▼ Monkeys can learn tricks.

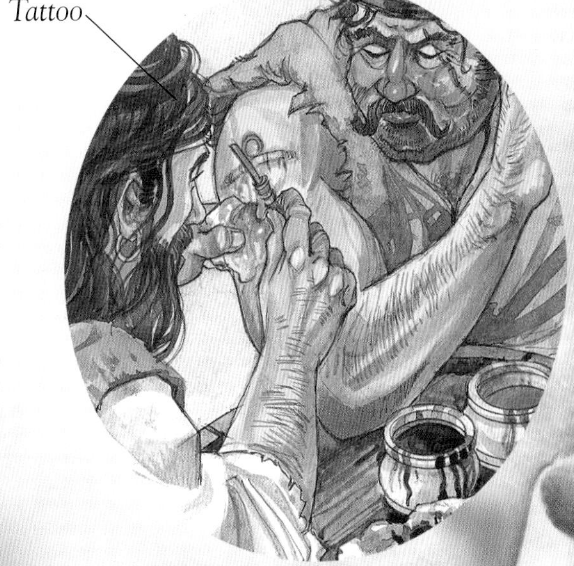
Tattoo

Punishment

As long as you are on board the *Dolphin* you follow the Ship's Articles. If you break the rules you will be punished, which is usually by flogging. The Quartermaster will whip your back with a cat-o'-nine-tails. This will cut your back to ribbons. Another punishment is keel-hauling, where the unfortunate seaman is dragged under water from one side of the ship to the other. If he survives, the half-drowned man may well die from the cuts he got as his body was pulled over the razor sharp barnacles which grow on the ship's hull.

Hanging

◀ Pray that you are never caught and 'turned off the cart'. This is an expression that means death by hanging.

Thirty-four...

▼ The cat-o'-nine-tails is made by the man to be flogged, as part of his punishment.

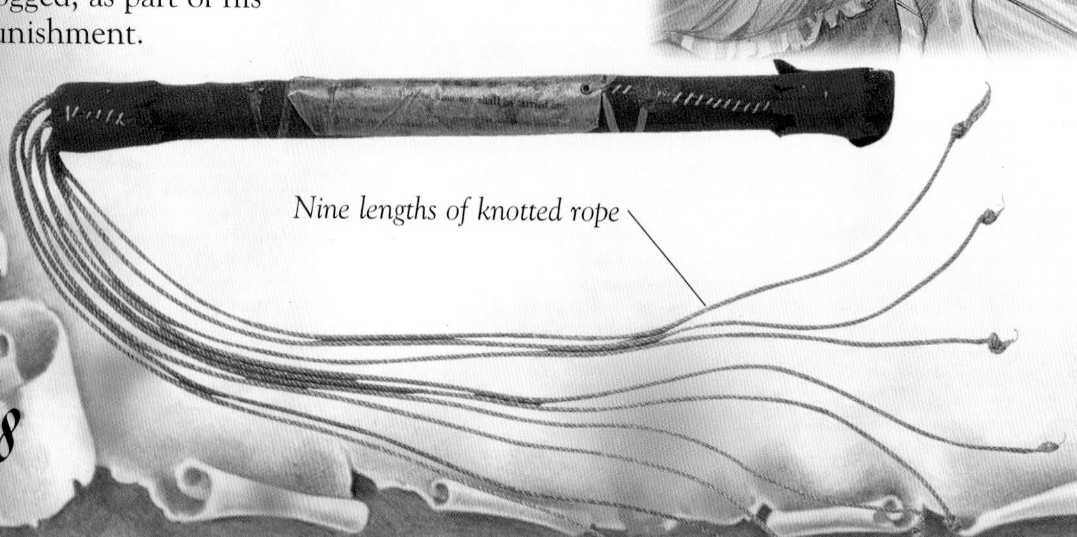

Nine lengths of knotted rope

Torture

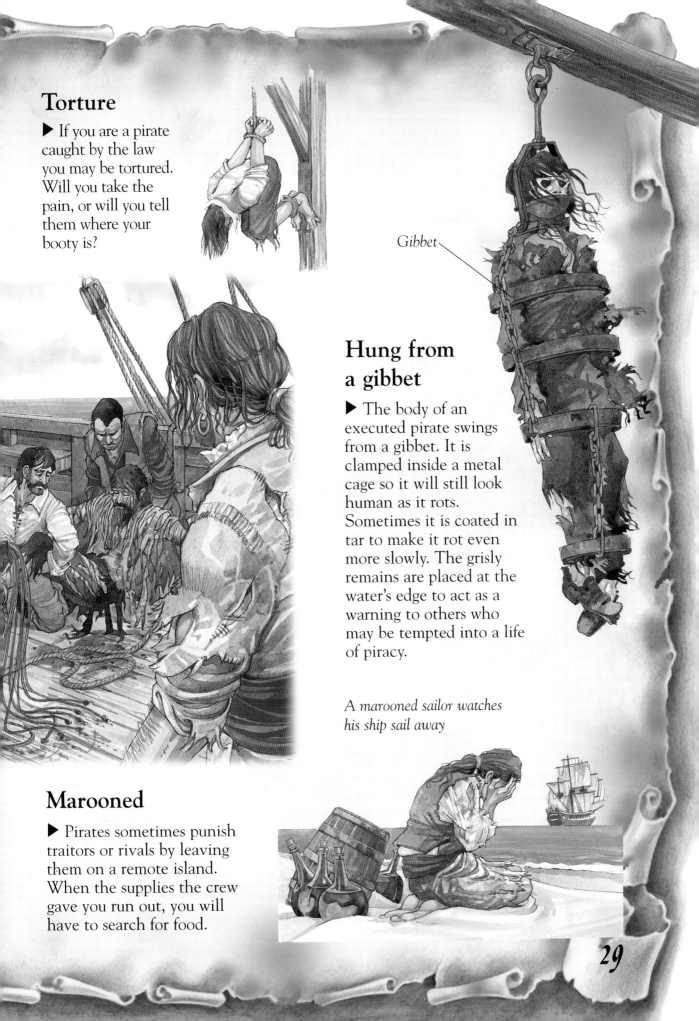

▶ If you are a pirate caught by the law you may be tortured. Will you take the pain, or will you tell them where your booty is?

Hung from a gibbet

▶ The body of an executed pirate swings from a gibbet. It is clamped inside a metal cage so it will still look human as it rots. Sometimes it is coated in tar to make it rot even more slowly. The grisly remains are placed at the water's edge to act as a warning to others who may be tempted into a life of piracy.

Gibbet

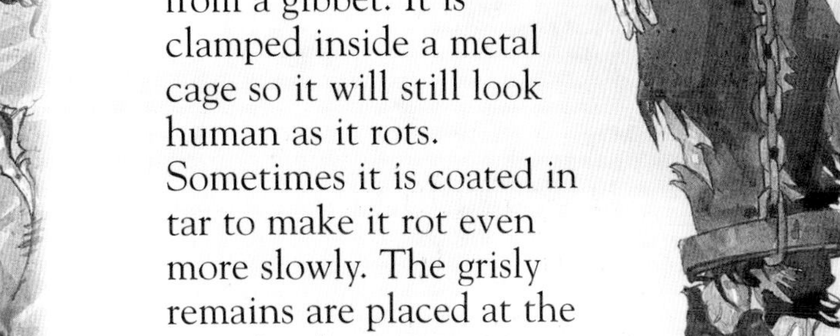

A marooned sailor watches his ship sail away

Marooned

▶ Pirates sometimes punish traitors or rivals by leaving them on a remote island. When the supplies the crew gave you run out, you will have to search for food.

Your Interview

Answer these questions to test your knowledge, then look at page 32 to find out if you have what it takes to get the job.

Q1 What are musket balls made of?
A Gold
B Silver
C Lead

Q2 What is a bowline?
A A knot
B A weapon
C A dance

Q3 How do you use tobacco on ship?
A Smoke it
B Chew it
C Wear it

Q4 What type of songs will you sing?
A Shanties
B Jigs
C Reels

Q5 What is salamagundi?
A Clothing
B A spiced stew
C A type of torture

Q6 What do you do with 'hard tack'?
A Fire it from your pistol
B Stamp on it before it bites
C Eat it

Q7 What is keel-hauling?
A Being dragged around the deck
B Being dragged under the ship
C Being dragged to the top of the mast

Q8 Who is second in command?
A The Quartermaster
B The musician
C You

Glossary

Backstaff A tool for working out the position of a ship.

Bilges The lowest compartment of a ship.

Booty Stolen goods.

Bow The front of a ship.

Bristol fashion A sailor's term for tidy.

Cat-o'-nine-tails A whip used for flogging.

Cutlass A pirate's sword.

Doubloon Spanish gold coin.

Galleon A large merchant ship.

Hold The area used for stores and sleeping quarters under the deck.

Knot A unit of measurement for a ship's speed.

Lip-plug An ornament worn in a hole cut through the lower lip.

Marooned To be abandoned.

Mutiny When the crew overrule the Captain and take control of their ship.

New World North and South America in relation to Europe.

Oakum Shredded rope used for sealing gaps in the ship's hull.

Piece-of-eight The nickname for a Spanish eight *reales* silver coin.

Pitch A black, resin-like liquid.

Privateer A type of pirate ship whose crew works for a government.

Prize ship A ship taken as wages or a reward.

Sailcloth Tough canvas for sails. Also used for making hard-wearing clothes.

Shot Small lead pellets used in shotguns.

Sloop A small, fast sailing ship.

Stern The back of a ship.

Tar Boiled-down pitch. Also a slang name for a sailor.

Tattoo A picture drawn into the skin, which is then permanent.

Index

Have you got the job?

Count up your correct answers (below right) and find out if you got the job.

Your score:

8 Congratulations: a pirate's life is obviously the one for you.
7 Not quite ready: but if someone drops out before the *Dolphin* leaves port, you can join us.
5-6 Promising: you have the right qualities – try again when we're back in port.
3-4 Not ready yet: your sea-legs are too shaky.
3 or less Too bad: you're only fit for fish food.

If you a life at sea is for you, read these books too:
Danger Zone: Avoid being a Pirates' Prisoner!
Danger Zone: Avoid sailing on a 19th-century Whaling Ship!
Danger Zone: Avoid sailing on the Titanic!
Danger Zone: Avoid sailing in the Spanish Armada!
Danger Zone: Avoid sailing with Christopher Columbus!
Inside the Beagle with Charles Darwin

1 (C) page 18
2 (A) page 9
3 (B) page 25
4 (A) page 8
5 (B) page 23
6 (C) page 23
7 (B) page 28
8 (A) page 11